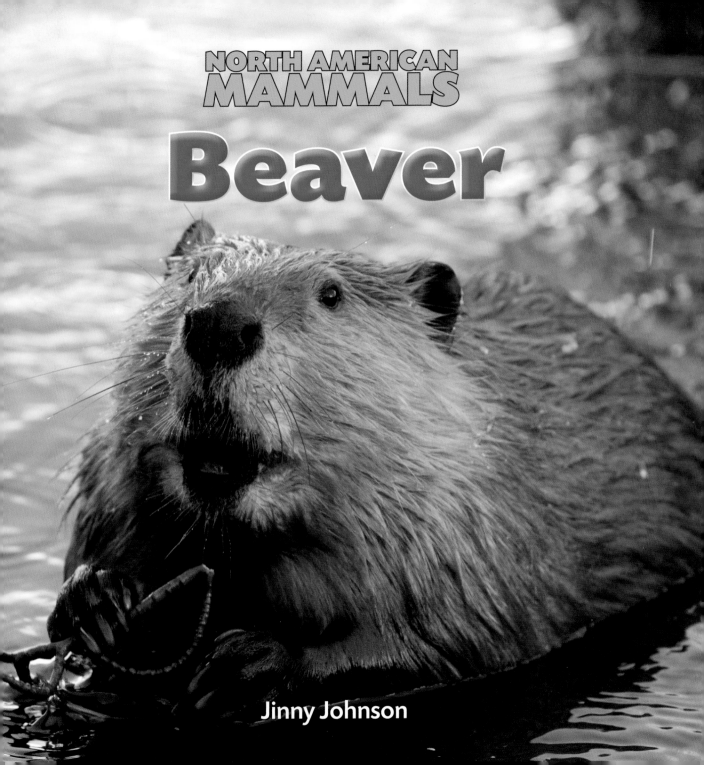

NORTH AMERICAN MAMMALS
Beaver

Jinny Johnson

Published by Smart Apple Media,
an imprint of Black Rabbit Books
P.O. Box 3263, Mankato, Minnesota, 56002
www.blackrabbitbooks.com

Printed in the United States of America,
at Corporate Graphics in North Mankato, Minnesota.

Designed by Hel James
Edited by Mary-Jane Wilkins

Library of Congress Cataloging-in-Publication Data

Johnson, Jinny, 1949-
  Beaver / Jinny Johnson.
     p. cm. -- (North American mammals)
  Includes index.
  ISBN 978-1-62588-031-4
  1. Beavers--North America--Juvenile literature. 2. Beavers--
Behavior--North America--Juvenile literature. I. Title.
  QL737.R632J64 2014
  599.37--dc23
                                    2013000064

Photo acknowledgements
t = top, b = bottom
title page Daniel Rose/Shutterstock; page 3 Gail Johnson/
Shutterstock; page 4 Brian Lasenby/Shutterstock;
5, 6 iStockphoto/Thinkstock; 7 Tom & Pat Leeson/ardea.com;
8 claffra/Shutterstock; 9t iStockphoto/Thinkstock, b David P.
Lewis/Shutterstock; 10 iStockphoto/Thinkstock; 11 NHPA/
Photoshot; 12 Francois Gohier/ardea.com; 13 fotofactory/
Shutterstock; 14 iStockphoto/Thinkstock; 15 Ammit Jack/
Shutterstock; 16 iStockphoto/Thinkstock; 17 Krzysztof Wiktor;
18 3483253554/Shutterstock; 19 iStockphoto/Thinkstock;
20 Alan Jeffery/Shutterstock; Joseph DiGrazia/Shutterstock;
22 Vladimir Chernyanskiy/Shutterstock; 23t basel101658,
b Gail Johnson/both Shutterstock
Cover Tania Thomson/Shutterstock

DAD0509
052013
9 8 7 6 5 4 3 2 1

Contents

Building a Dam   4

Our Home   6

Favorite Foods   8

Swimming   10

Diving   12

Keeping Warm   14

Busy Beavers   16

Lots to Learn   18

Leaving Home   20

Beaver Facts   22

Useful Words   24

Index   24

I am a beaver.

I like to live where there are lots of trees and plenty of water.

Building a Dam

Did you know that beavers are expert builders?

We make a dam across
a stream to make a
quiet pond where
we can build our home.

We use logs, branches,
and mud to make
the dam.

Our Home

Our home is called a lodge and it's built of sticks and mud. It's warm and sheltered, even in winter.

Our living area is above the water, but the entrances are under water.

I was born in our lodge and I live there with my parents and younger brothers and sisters.

Favorite Foods

Our favorite foods are tree bark, twigs, leaves, and roots. We have big sharp teeth for stripping bark from trees and chewing our food.

Our front teeth just keep growing and they never wear out. They are so strong that we can cut down quite big trees.

9

Swimming

I can move around on land quite well, but I'm much happier in the water.

I'm a very good swimmer and I use my webbed back feet to help me move along.

I steer myself with my flat, paddle-shaped tail. If I see any signs of danger, such as a wolf or a coyote, I slap the water with my tail to warn the rest of the family.

Diving

I'm an expert diver too and sometimes I stay underwater for as long as 15 minutes. I can close off my nose and ears so I don't get water in them.

I have see-through eyelids.
I can close my eyes but
still see where I'm going
when I'm diving.

13

Keeping Warm

The water can get cold
in winter, but my two layers
of fur keep me toasty warm.

The outer layer of fur is waterproof and I groom it every day so it stays that way.

I have special claws on each back foot that I use to comb and clean my fur.

Busy Beavers

We usually rest in the lodge during the day and start work after dark.

16

Every night we
check the dam
and lodge and
make any repairs.
We really are
busy beavers.

We spend a good
deal of time finding
food and eating, too.

Lots to Learn

My mom and dad are teaching me all I need to know about finding food and building dams and lodges.

Leaving Home

When I'm about
two years old,
I will leave my
parents' lodge.

I will find a mate
and we will make
a dam and build
our own home.

Beaver Facts

The American beaver lives in parts of North America, from Alaska to Mexico. It belongs to the rodent group of mammals and it is the largest rodent in North America.

Beavers live in family groups of mother, father, and young of different ages. Young beavers are called kits.

A beaver is about 24-32 inches (60-82 cm) long with a tail of 10-18 inches (25-46 cm). It weighs 35-65 pounds (16-30 kg).

Beavers make their home in water so it is harder for land predators to reach them.

4 feet (1.2 m)

4 feet (1.2 m); height of average 7-year-old

Beavers also live in parts of Asia and Europe.

23

Useful Words

groom To care for and clean the fur.

predator An animal that lives by hunting and killing other animals.

webbed A webbed foot has skin between the toes to help the animal swim.

Index

claws 15

dams 4, 5, 16, 17, 19, 21

diving 12, 13

ears 12

eyes 13

feet 10, 15
food 8, 9, 17, 18, 19

fur 14, 15

grooming 15, 24

lodges 6, 7, 16, 17, 18, 19, 21

mud 5, 6

nose 12

swimming 10, 11

tail 11, 23
teeth 8, 9

Web Link

Learn more about beavers at: http://kids.nationalgeographic.com/kids/animals/creaturefeature/beavers